Forgiveness

Sharing
Emotions

Guilt

Being Realistic

Memories

Being Impulsive

Empathy

Vengeance

I Know Myself

Assertiveness

A Child's Book of
Emotions

A Child's Book of Emotions
Originally published in Spain as
El Gran Libro de las Emociones

Editor: Jesús Araújo
Texts: Esteve Pujol i Pons and Rafael Bisquerra Alzina
Illustrations: Carles Arbat
Design and page makeup: Jordi Martínez
Production: Sagrafic, S.L.

First edition: August 2012
© Copyright 2012 Parramón Paidotribo. World Rights
Published by Parramón Paidotribo, S.L., Badalona, Spain
English-language edition copyright © 2014 by Paulist Press, Inc.

Library of Congress Control Number: 2014936649

ISBN: 978-0-8091-6772-2

Published by Paulist Press
997 Macarthur Boulevard
Mahwah, New Jersey 07430

www.paulistpress.com

Printed in China

A Child's Book of
Emotions

Texts by Esteve Pujol i Pons
and Rafael Bisquerra Alzina

Illustrations by Carles Arbat

PAULIST PRESS
New York / Mahwah, NJ

Contents

Introduction
From me...I want to go... toward others....

You're very likely to be a boy or girl who wants to live happily with everyone else, who wants to have fun with your friends. You want them to accept you in their groups and want to be with you. You know that all this is not always easy.

In each story, you'll discover a little secret that will help you to get along better with those around you.

In part one of the book, FROM ME..., there are stories with ideas on how you should behave, and how to become aware of what you are like, of your qualities, of the emotions you feel; how to keep yourself from being overcome by anger or fear; how to appreciate the good things in life; how to avoid becoming sad when things don't work out as you would like; how it's better to be happy and not sad....

In part two, called I WANT TO GO…, some very beautiful stories will inspire you to move forward, despite difficulties. Everyone encounters obstacles and setbacks. The stories' characters show how their very strong wills enable them to continue on their paths decisively, steadily, and bravely.

And in part three, TOWARD OTHERS…, you will find some brilliant ideas for getting along better with others: with your family or your group of friends, wherever you happen to be. You will learn ways to act that will make your relationships as good as possible. For, as you know, there are certain ways of behaving that make others like you, and others that do just the opposite. Some make everyone happier. Some are worth doing; others should be avoided.

FROM ME...I WANT TO GO...TOWARD OTHERS: from yourself, as you are...you want to get closer...to others..., in order to have good relationships with them.

It is very important that you like the stories. You can ask the grown-ups in your house to read or explain them to you. Don't worry if you don't understand some of the words at the beginning or end of each story. Your family or teachers can help you to understand them properly, you'll see.

Have fun!

I Know Myself

When you say, "I know myself," and mean it, you are referring to what is called "emotional intelligence." It is nothing other than the ability to be aware of your own emotions. It is not a question of being content, or furious, or irritated, but of being aware that you are content or furious or irritated. What's more, emotional intelligence also means knowing whether or not it is appropriate to deal with certain delicate questions at a particular time.

This is the basic, essential element of emotional intelligence: I know myself and I know others. Without this, it is impossible to reach others in a socially intelligent way. First, "I know myself"; the rest can come later.

Tom Thumb

Popular Tale

Once upon a time, there was a tiny boy who was very short but very lively. His name was Tom Thumb. He always wanted to do everything by himself, but his father and mother wouldn't let him. "Tom Thumb, you are too small," they would tell him.

The boy would reply, "You don't need to do everything for me. I can do plenty of things on my own."

One day his mother said, "We have no bread left to eat."

"I'll go to the baker's to buy a loaf," offered Tom Thumb.

"Don't you see, you're too small? Why, someone could tread upon you in the street!" his father pointed out.

"Then I'll sing so loud that everyone will notice me," replied Tom Thumb, who always had an answer for everything.

At the bakery, the woman behind the counter was startled when she heard a little voice ask for a loaf of bread. Looking around, she saw no one.

"Don't be afraid," Tom Thumb said. "I am down here, in front of the counter, and I want a loaf of bread."

He sang and whistled the whole way home so that no one would step on him by accident.

Tom Thumb's father was a waiter. One day he reached work and realized he'd forgotten the pills he took every day after lunch for his high blood pressure. He rang his wife to ask her to bring them. Tom Thumb answered the phone. "Don't worry, Father, I'll bring you the pills. I know where they are."

"No, Tom Thumb, the road is too dangerous—it has a lot of bends and is very busy with cars," his father told him.

"You'll see, I'll be there at once."

As he was crossing the fields, a terrible storm broke out, and it started to rain cats and dogs. Tom Thumb took refuge under a cabbage in a garden and fell asleep. When he awoke, there was no cabbage. An ox had eaten it! Thankfully, the pills were safe, and Tom Thumb hurried to the restaurant.

His father was surprised when he saw his son arrive, smiling and not at all wet.

"You see, Father," said Tom Thumb, more pleased with himself than ever, "being as small as a chickadee doesn't mean that I can't do the same things as other boys my age. You believe in me now, don't you?"

The embrace of his father was reward enough for Tom Thumb, whose courage made all things possible.

The End

Knowing our own emotions, how we are feeling, is important. We cannot relate to others unless we know what we are feeling.

Tom Thumb trusted himself because he had a positive self-image. He was aware of his limitations and fears, but his confidence about his strengths enabled him to find solutions to his problems.

Naming Emotions

When you can put a name on something, you know more about it. If you can put a name on what you are feeling, on your emotions, then you understand your emotions better and you gain some control over those feelings.

You can make a list of emotions, as if you were a "collector of emotions." Beside each emotion, write down its definition, its advantages and disadvantages, and the concrete situations where you have experienced it: in real life or in fiction (books, film, television…).

Having and using a rich and varied emotional language will help you to know yourself better.

The Pied Piper of Hamelin

The Brothers Grimm (Germany)

The city of Hamelin suffered an invasion of rats that terrified both young and old. Rats appeared everywhere: in houses, in granaries, in shops, and in the streets. They were simply everywhere!

"What are the mayor and councilors doing?" the villagers shouted. "Can't they see that this vermin will devour everything in our pantries, as well as our entire harvest? They might even eat our children and us!"

The mayor responded to the complaints of the townspeople by promising fifty-thousand gold pieces to anyone who managed to exterminate the rats and rid Hamelin of this terrible problem. A few days later, a tall, thin man carrying a flute under his arm appeared at the Town Hall.

"I know how to free the city of Hamelin of its rats and mice," he told the Town Council.

"Wonderful!" the mayor replied enthusiastically. "When there's not a single rodent left, we will give you the promised reward."

The piper began to play a magical tune on his flute, weaving this way and that throughout the entire city. To everyone's surprise, the rats streamed out of the houses, the granaries, and the shops. They crawled out of their deepest, darkest hiding places, and followed him as if spellbound by the mysterious tune. When they reached the fast-flowing River Weser, which crosses Hamelin, the piper stood still in front of the mass of rats, playing his music with even greater intensity. At once, all of the rats leapt into the river's rushing waters and drowned!

"Mayor, councilors, citizens of Hamelin, I have fulfilled my part of the agreement. Now you must fulfill yours."

"Here! Here!" the Mayor answered. "Thank you, my dear piper, for eliminating the rats. But we think that just blowing on your pipe was too easy for us to simply hand over fifty-thousand gold pieces. One hundred gold pieces, don't you agree, seems payment enough."

"We agreed upon fifty thousand and so it should be fifty thousand. Remember, my dear mayor," the rat hunter replied in irritation, "you gave me your word."

When the mayor refused, the piper picked up his pipe, and started to play another enchanting song. This time, instead of rats

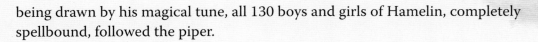

being drawn by his magical tune, all 130 boys and girls of Hamelin, completely spellbound, followed the piper.

When he was a long way from Hamelin, the piper played another tune, this one the most mesmerizing of all. The piper's song led the children into a cleft in a mountainside. One by one, the children marched in. Then, at a sharp whistle, the mountain closed, leaving them all trapped inside.

The inhabitants of Hamelin wailed in desperation. They knew they had been unjust, miserly, deceitful, cowardly, and selfish. The mayor and the councilors begged the piper to forgive them and take pity on them. They then offered him double: 100,000 gold pieces. The musician thought that the offer was excellent and gladly accepted it. He even admitted that his punishment may have been a bit excessive, and released the children to their families.

From then on, the villagers of Hamelin wondered about the mysterious piper with his magic flute, and how they came close to losing their loved ones because of greed, while their children played in streets without a rat in sight.

The End

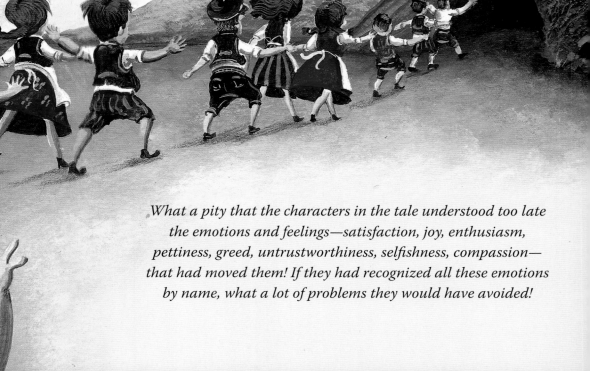

What a pity that the characters in the tale understood too late the emotions and feelings—satisfaction, joy, enthusiasm, pettiness, greed, untrustworthiness, selfishness, compassion— that had moved them! If they had recognized all these emotions by name, what a lot of problems they would have avoided!

Self-Control

Managing your emotions appropriately can also be called self-control, regulation, or emotional control.

Some people always exaggerate their emotions and others always hide them. The best way is between the two extremes. You have to take into account the context you are in to determine to what extent feelings and emotions should be shown. An expression of joy or loud laughter in one situation may be inappropriate in another.

The balanced person fits their emotions to the situation and does not let their emotions control their behavior.

The Tortoise and the Eagle

A Fable by Aesop (Ancient Greece)

Once upon a time, when animals talked, there was a tortoise called Slowcoach who lived on the shore of Lake All-Is-Water. Like all tortoises, she walked slowly, for she had to carry her heavy shell on her back. One day she decided that she wanted to go to the opposite side of the lake. "Perhaps," she said to herself, "I will find tastier food there." In order to make such a long trip, though, she knew she would need to devote a great deal of time and effort.

An eagle with shiny feathers, powerful claws, and a strong beak flew down to drink beside Slowcoach.

"Good day," the tortoise said. "What is your name, royal bird?"

"Good day, tortoise," the eagle replied. "I'm called Swift Flight, because I fly very fast!"

"Listen, Swift Flight," Slowcoach replied. "Can you do me a huge favor? I want to go to the other side of the lake. Do you think you could take me there?"

"I don't like the idea too much," the eagle replied. "I would clutch you in my claws and hurt you."

"Pick up a tree branch with your feet," Slowcoach said, "with one claw holding each end, and I'll hang in the middle of the branch with my beak, which is very strong."

The eagle agreed, and soon the tortoise was hanging from the tree branch by her beak and passing over the water as if she, too, were a bird in the sky.

"Slowcoach," Swift Flight asked, "I have to ask, why do you have such an ugly name? And why do you have a shell that you must carry around with you and always slows you down?"

Slowcoach felt offended by Swift Flight's words, especially when Swift Flight added, "And what's more, you're always acting scared. When you see danger, you hide in your shell like a coward!"

Slowcoach became more and more enraged. What pleasure did Swift Flight find in mocking her?

"Look at me!" Swift Flight went on. "My body is elegant and handsome. What wings, what feathers, what a beak, what eyes! My sharp claws are good for hunting and eating. And I can fly any distance I wish to in no time. I am the Queen of the birds!"

Slowcoach's rage filled her. Anger clouded her thoughts. She would give this bird a piece of her mind! She would tell this bird what's what!

"Look—"

When Slowcoach, without thinking, opened her beak to shout the first word, she let go of the tree branch to which she had been clinging.

And with that, poor, unfortunate Slowcoach fell like a stone. The slap as she hit the water echoed to the shores of the lake. She drowned because land tortoises, as you know, do not know how to swim.

The End

Slowcoach did not know how to control her feeling of anger at the insults of Swift Flight: emotion dominated her. If she had controlled herself, if she had kept quiet when she should have, she could have answered Swift Flight after she had put her down on the other side of the lake. She was unable to control her anger at a critical moment and this had fatal consequences for her.

Enjoying Beauty

Aesthetic emotions are those experienced when we see the beauty of nature, human actions, and works of art (literature, painting, sculpture, architecture, music, dance, film…). These emotions provide a sensation of happiness, they satisfy our souls. It's a good idea to learn to enjoy aesthetic emotions and to encourage those experiences that will increase our social and personal happiness.

My Friend Blenka

A Story about Inuit Culture (Canada)

In mid-May, I reached Kuujjuarapik, a Canadian city of a thousand inhabitants on the Labrador Peninsula, on the east coast of the Hudson Bay, beside the mouth of the Great Whale River. I met Blenka, who was to be my guide for a week in those icy, but marvelously beautiful lands.

"Welcome to the land of the Inuits!" she said, greeting me.

"Thank you, Blenka! I thought it was the land of the Eskimos," I replied.

"We don't much like being called Eskimos. In truth, we are Inuits, an ethnic group that has lived for over 2,800 years in the Arctic, from the steppes of Siberia in the West to Greenland, passing through Alaska and Canada. Call us Inuits, please."

During the days in which we crossed that Northern land, Blenka and I had many great conversations.

One morning I said to her, "Blenka, don't you find so much whiteness monotonous?" We were faced with kilometers of immaculate snow, only broken by spots of moss and some isolated rocks.

"Do you, then, see it as all white?" she asked with a gleam in her eyes. "We see an infinite variety of whites, you know. We Inuits have over forty words to name what you just call snow. If I wanted to translate them, I would say that

we have the following whites of snow: shining, ashy, celestial, walrus reflection, young bear skin, bright morning, cloudy morning, clean dusk, dark dusk, afternoon storm, disturbed water, the light of dawn….So you understand, you just see white and you find it boring; if I just saw white, I'd find it boring, too."

"And this total silence?" I asked another day. "Isn't it overwhelming?"

"Overwhelming?" she answered. "If it was true silence, perhaps, but it isn't. Listen carefully and you will hear the many different whispers that the wind makes. Do you hear them? Now the wind's more powerful than a few minutes ago…and now it's not so loud. Also, have you heard the distant murmur of the ocean? Or the roar of a mother bear calling for her cub? And that noise, far in the background? Why, that is a storm drawing near. Here we say, 'How the sun shines!' or 'See you tomorrow!' in hundreds of different tones….With this 'silence' I never feel alone!"

"You said that 'the sun shines.' How can you get used to summer days with no nights and winters with no day?"

"Look," she said with a fascinating smile. "Do you know what joy it is to see the sun swinging through the sky and the earth never able to swallow it, and then just when it seems about to disappear, it rises back up, not leaving us for a moment? And this perpetual night you mention gives us long hours of beautiful sleep. It is as if all of nature went to sleep, dreaming of precious pasts and hopeful futures. During this 'darkness,' the figures carved of seal bone or walrus tusks are born.

The artist carves and polishes them, focused and unhurried, because he or she knows that the morning will be a long time in coming."

When I returned to my country, I began to understand that beauty was different for everyone and is perhaps best captured with the heart, and that in order to enjoy beauty, first I must learn its language.

A minimum of training and education in art helps us appreciate beauty.

Blenka perceives beauty, which makes her happy, where the rest of us may only experience boredom and lack of interest.

Being Impulsive

When you are impulsive, you have no control over your emotions. The person who manages his/her emotions does not behave impulsively, because he/she thinks before acting. It is important to know how to leave a space between thought and action...like counting to ten or even a hundred before we act on our feelings when faced with an unexpected reaction.

Knowing yourself allows you to realize how impulsive you can be when you feel strong emotions, such as irritation, anger, rage, and absolute joy

Though it may be hard, you have to be able to reflect before acting impulsively.

Don Rodrigo's Dog

A Tale from Calila e Dimna (13th Century Spain)

Once upon a time, there was a count named Don Rodrigo, who went out on a tour of all of his lands, accompanied by his gentlemen and servants. Before going out, he told his dog (for he was a man who talked to his dog), "Valiant, I'm going to inspect my land. Stay at the castle and do what I tell you. My son Arnulfo is asleep in his cradle. Watch him well, and don't let anything bad happen to him. I'll be back soon."

Don Rodrigo petted the dog, which was white with spots of brown. He loved Valiant a great deal. The dog had lived in his house for many years, and he was a faithful and obedient mastiff. As soon as the count left the castle with his entire retinue of nobles and servants, a hungry wolf with silvery fur and a black throat found a door of the castle ajar and slipped inside. His nose led him to a most delicious smell, and soon he was climbing the stairs to the room where little

Arnulfo was sound asleep. When he poked his pointed muzzle through the bedroom door, he saw Valiant, who stood guard by the little babe with his ears pricked and his sharp teeth showing as if to say, "Wolf, here you will not pass. I will defend my master's son, and I'll do it with my teeth. You'd better flee!"

The wolf paused for a moment, then lowered his head and calculated distances, showed his terrible teeth, and flashed his eyes at the dog. He leapt at Valiant, who stood his ground. A horrible fight between wolf and dog began. They were so embroiled in the struggle that Arnulfo's cradle was knocked over and the sheets were stained with the blood of both animals. The fight was so cruel that Valiant wounded the wolf mortally, while he fell badly injured beside the cradle.

Count Don Rodrigo returned, very satisfied with his outing, and went up to see his son. Imagine his fright when he saw the cradle overturned and the bedclothes red with blood! He searched for his son and could not find him! What he found was Valiant with blood on his jaws and all over his body, lying beside the cradle. Anger shook him from head to toe and made him unsheathe his sword, grasp it with rage, and plunge it deep into the body of Valiant, while he roared in his madness, "You've killed my son! Die, wretch!"

The shout awoke Arnulfo, who was sleeping, half hidden, on the other side of his cradle. His crying drew the attention of his despairing father, who went to him, lifted him up from the floor, covered him with kisses, and soaked him with tears of joy.

What had happened? The count soon understood everything. He owed his son's life to the courage of Valiant, his great and faithful dog. The tears were then of repentance for having understood his own impulsiveness too late.

Think before acting, because afterward there is no way back.

What a pity that Don Rodrigo didn't take a few moments to calm down and discover what had really happened. If he hadn't acted impulsively, he and Arnulfo would have shown their gratitude to Valiant for the rest of his life; and Valiant would have been their companion and protected them for a long time.

Anger

Anger is a basic emotion that shows itself in many different ways and has many different names: rage, irritation, indignation, hatred, and so on. The word *anger* is used to refer to all of these feelings.

Anger is one of the most dangerous emotions, since it causes violent behavior of many kinds: insults, provocation, blows, hurting, killing, and the like. Violence is often the consequence of impulsiveness when we are angry.

Emotions are not good or bad: we just feel them. What we *do* with them is good or bad. If in anger we shout, insult, or hurt, we are using anger in a damaging way. However, anger in the face of injustice is perfectly legitimate and has to be directed into constructing a more just world, but never through violence.

The Elephant and the Rain God

A Tale from the Maasai People (Africa)

Many, many years ago, on the plains of the Lossogonoi, which is east of central Africa in what is now Tanzania, there lived an arrogant elephant who believed he was the king. When he raised his formidable head, he could make out the snowy peaks of Kilimanjaro. When he walked about, all the other animals obeyed his commands.

The Lossogonoi was an immense green valley with lush grass inhabited by insects and reptiles, with plants and thickets where all kinds of animals lived and trees in which all the birds nested. The waters of the River Pangani irrigated the plain, fell in thunderous waterfalls, and formed the vast pools of Nyumbaya.

Baial, God of rain, caused the rain to fall generously on that African region. One day the elephant confronted Baial, with whom he maintained an ancient rivalry, and told him, "Who do you think you are? What would you do if I tore up the grass, the plants, and the thickets, if I destroyed the trees of Lossogonoi, and everything was reduced to a desert?"

Baial was annoyed by the insolence of the elephant and replied, "Don't you see, vain and stupid beast, that you would be left with nothing to eat and you would die of hunger, along with all the animals of the plain?"

The elephant, enraged by the rain god's reply, started to tear up the grass, the plants, the thickets, and the trees until the Lossogonoi had no vegetation left at all.

Baial exploded in anger and decided not to let rain fall ever again on that land. The Lossogonoi became arid, the Pangani turned into nothing more than a wretched stream, and the animals began dying of hunger and thirst.

The elephant, contemplating the disaster that his pride and bad temper had caused, went to see Baial. He asked him to let it rain again on the thirsty plain, but Baial was irritated and took no notice of him. The drought became even more suffocating.

Then the elephant, remembering that the cock was a good friend of Baial, as each morning it woke up the Sun, asked him to intercede so that it would rain again.

"Baial, majestic God of the rain, stop being angry at the elephant. Now he has repented and promises he will not talk disrespectfully to you again. The Lossogonoi is dying of hunger and thirst; soon all life will disappear. Allow it to rain with abundance, and the plants and animals will be eternally grateful to you."

Baial became less angry and made it rain again, but much less than before. The water formed a single pool, and the elephant took control of it at once. When he had quenched his thirst, he ordered the tortoise not to let anyone drink when he wasn't there because the pond was his alone.

At first, everything went fine for the tortoise. The animals that approached were small and could be easily sent away. But things changed when the lion arrived, looking for a drink of water.

"I am the lion and I can do what I like!" he roared in indignation before giving the tortoise a swat with his mighty paw that hurled it far away. Then the lion drank all the water he wanted. And after him, the other animals did the same.

When the elephant returned, imagine how furious he was when he saw they had drunk his water.

The tortoise, who had been left lying on her back, apologized, "Mr. Elephant, I am a weak animal, so the stronger ones ignore me. What could poor little me do? What's more, the lion has injured me by a blow from his paw and left me lying on my back."

The elephant was so furious that he raised a foot and brought it down with all his strength on the tortoise's shell. Ever since that day, if you'll notice, the tortoise's shell is flat underneath.

When the God of rain saw what had happened, his temper grew hot. But he knew he must try to calm himself down. When he had, he addressed all the animals of the Lossogonoi:

"My friends, do not behave like the elephant, who has abused his strength and challenged the inhabitants of the Lossogonoi plain and the Pangani River. Rage and hatred only bring hunger and wretchedness, pain and death. Share what you have and don't try to keep everything for yourselves alone. I hope we've learned our lesson well!"

Then Baial made the waters fall abundantly once more, and the Lossogonoi again became a beautiful green valley, with lush grass

inhabited by insects and reptiles, with plants and thickets where all kinds of animals lived, with trees in which all the birds nested, and where the fast-flowing Pangani River ran.

The End

Our anger leads us to violence, which brings great problems for everyone. The animals in the tale, including the rain god himself, let themselves be driven by anger and all kinds of evil events followed.

It is important to accept the feeling of anger and, if necessary, convert it into noble anger against injustice, but it should never drift into hatred, violence, or new injustice.

Fear

Fear is a basic emotion that we feel in different ways, such as dread, terror, horror, and panic. When we are afraid, our most primary, instinctive behavior is to run away.

It is useful to distinguish between fear and anxiety. Fear is suffered before a real, imminent danger, such as a fire, a natural disaster, or a predator; whereas anxiety is experienced before a danger that *could* happen but is not likely to happen. It is characterized by the thought "what if...": what if I fall, what if something happens to my family, what if they keep me in during recess, what if....

Anxiety is much more common than fear in our society. The distinction is important, since in the case of fear, you have to make sure you survive the danger; whereas, in the case of anxiety, you have to quiet yourself down and not overreact to something that you are worrying about but most likely won't happen.

The Two Brave Tailors

"Rondalla" by Jacint Verdaguer (Catalonia, Spain)

Once upon a time, there were some rich farmers from the village of Sora who asked two tailors from Sant Boi de Lluçanès to make them some suits. The tailors planned to travel by night, so that at dawn, they would have arrived and could get to work very early. Thus they left Sant Boi at dusk, each of them carrying the tools of his trade in his pack, everything they needed to cut and sew a suit.

The path was very narrow, full of rough stretches between oaks, dirt, and rocks. Soon it was dark. All kinds of owls filled the air with hoots and gloomy wheezing and cries. The two tailors, scared by the constant racket and mysterious dark shadows that were moving all round them, came across a white silhouette as tall as a man in the middle of the path. Wondering whether it was a real person or a ghost, they stopped short. They trembled and whispered to each other about what they could do. Their panic was so enormous that their tongues were tied and their arms and legs were paralyzed as if they had been frozen from head to toe. It was as if that white figure was saying to them, "Here I await you. Whatever you do, you will have to pass through here. You cannot escape."

At last, one of the tailors whispered to the other in a thin ribbon of a voice, "It's the goat-man, the terrible bandit of the Guilleries! The one who just last week drove off an entire battalion of soldiers that was after him! Now we really are doomed!"

"But, if it's not him?" the other replied.

"How could it not be him?" the other responded. "Don't you see how the double-barreled shotgun he uses to terrify the whole county glints in the moonlight? If he raises it, woe on us! A barrel load for each of us!"

"Horrible," the other whispered. "He's just one and there are two of us, but even if there were ten of us, he'd shoot us for his breakfast! What if we asked him to let us through?"

"Try it, but above all, don't irritate him."

Going up to the white silhouette, the tailor said in a tremulous voice, "A very good night to you, Sir. We are two tailors from Sant Boi on our way to Sora. Would you allow us to pass, please?"

Nothing at all. The white figure remained still and silent and seemed ever more threatening. The two tailors' clothes hardly touched their bodies, they shook so. Their teeth chattered and their hair stood on end.

"Go on, you tell him. Perhaps he'll pay more attention to you. He mustn't have heard me."

The other tailor repeated with a voice that hardly came out from the collar of his shirt, "A very good night to you, Sir. We are two tailors from Sant Boi on our way to Sora. Would you allow us to pass, please?"

But the white ghost continued to ignore them: not a gesture or a word. If the two tailors felt scared before asking him the question, they were terrified now. The ghost showed them not the slightest intention of letting them continue their journey, as he stood solid in the middle of the track, blocking their route.

For the third time, the tailors pleaded in a murmur that they themselves could hardly hear, "A very good night to you, Sir. We are two tailors from Sant Boi on our way to Sora. Would you allow us to pass, please?"

But the white thing was as deaf as he had been before. So the two tailors, intimidated and afraid of irritating the ghost if they persisted with their request, crouched down on the ground, clinging to a rock beside the track, keeping as quiet as they could. They would wait until daybreak to see whether the goat-man, the terrible bandit of the Guilleries, had left.

At the crack of dawn, the tailors opened their eyes and could hardly believe what they saw before them. Oh, how ashamed they felt! The white thing they had imagined was a murderer or a ghost and that wanted to eat them alive was just the trunk of a fat tree, white because it was so old, its bark peeled by cattle and rain, and the same height as a big man.

When they realized their mistake, the two heroes cheered up and suddenly felt infinitely courageous. One picked up a stick he found beside the path and, as if it were a sharp sword, hit that ancient trunk with rage. The other pulled out of his pack the enormous tailor's scissors and thrust them again and again into the heart of the trunk.

"Ah, if only you were a man! You'd have seen what's what if you were a man!"

The End

It is important to be calm so we can face life's challenges and do our best.

Fear put the tailors of the story in a ridiculous situation and, what's more, made them late in reaching their destination.

They were brave, but only with words and only when courage was no longer needed.

40

Sadness

Sadness is an emotion that we experience when we lose something valuable: an object, a game, an opportunity, and, above all, a loved one. Sadness covers many feelings, such as sorrow, pain, affliction, despondency, and dejection. When you're sad, you want to cry, relationships with others become difficult and you tend to turn in on yourself.

Sadness happens to everyone, since things we don't like happen to everyone. We cannot always win and, when we lose, we are sad.

We have to understand sadness in ourselves and in others and respect it. You have to let people cry when they are sad, if that is what they want. We can offer our help, while always respecting their privacy.

The Painter Notxa Was Sad

A Chinese Legend

Notxa was a small child who lived with his family in Qun-xin, a village in ancient China. He painted very well. The whole family said so, and even the villagers recognized his skill. He painted so well, in fact, that his reputation spread throughout China and reached the very palace of the Emperor.

"Great Imperial Lord," the palace steward began, "in Qun-xin, there is a lad who paints the most beautiful pictures we have ever seen. Not even the best painters of the Court paint like he does."

"Then I order that he be brought to the palace and paint only for me," the Emperor pronounced.

The imperial soldiers walked for seven days to reach the house of the young Notxa.

"His Imperial Majesty commands that you come to the palace and paint only for him."

Great sorrow filled Notxa's heart, for he was so young to leave his family and live far away at the Emperor's palace, but he had to obey the Emperor. He embraced his parents and brothers and left with tears in his eyes, accompanied by the soldiers.

He appeared before the Emperor, who told him in a solemn voice, "Notxa, I know you are an excellent painter. From now on, you will live in my palace. You will have a large room just for yourself. You will be provided with every color and everything you need to paint. I just place one condition on you: paint solely for me."

In that immense building, Notxa felt like a bird enclosed in a gilded cage. He was so sad that he couldn't draw a picture, not even a sketch. He recalled the country around Qun-xin and his beloved family and could not stop crying.

A palace servant, lively and pretty, called Miska, noticed Notxa's melancholy.

"I understand that you are so sad you cannot paint, my friend," she told him. "You have to pull yourself together, even if only for one picture. Cheer up, even if only this once."

Notxa took her advice. He dried his tears. He took a large canvas, brushes, and paints. He painted the most beautiful landscape you could imagine, with bright colors, soft undulations, some mountains in the background that stole your heart, where the forests were a curtain of green and the clouds sweetened the sky. It was the countryside he used to see each day when he stepped outside his home.

When the Emperor saw it, he ordered that it be hung in the throne room. Whoever saw it was captivated. They thought it a great window through which to look at Paradise.

But now Notxa's sadness was even deeper than before. He could not enter the throne room to see his picture. Only high dignitaries had access. One day, when the imperial guard was paying less attention than they normally do, he snuck into the throne room and took the picture. The Emperor was very upset. He ordered a search for the picture. On finding it hidden away in Notxa's room, he called the lad.

"Notxa," the Emperor said, taking pity on the boy's sadness, "I understand your sorrow. From now on, you can look at your picture one day a week for an hour."

Notxa did this for several weeks. Even though he still missed his family terribly, at least in that hour, gazing at his beautiful painting, his sadness was consoled.

One afternoon Miska said, "Notxa, I can't bear to see you suffer so. You have to paint as before. Why don't we escape together and go far away?"

"Miska, how do you think we can flee the Emperor's palace?
The doors are well guarded; the sentries watch the walls. It is
impossible for us to leave the palace without being arrested. The
punishment would be terrible; we'd be risking our lives."

"Think, Notxa," the girl insisted. "You artists always have brilliant ideas
and you more than anyone else."

For three days Notxa felt mixed sadness and optimism; his mind went over
ideas and strategies. At dusk on the third day, he said to Miska, "Listen
carefully. The day after tomorrow, after lunch, I will go and see my
picture. You must be there, too. You can go in because at that time
you are arranging the room for the meeting of the Imperial
Council."

When they met in the throne room and the other servants had
left, Notxa and Miska went as close to the canvas as they
could. They held hands and looked at the picture.
They approached so closely that they passed into
it, as if the picture had taken on life and absorbed
them. They flew over valleys and mountains, a very
long way: perhaps as far as Qun-xin.

Notxa recovered his happiness and started painting again. His pictures were more beautiful than ever. Miska, enraptured, admired the paintings...and him.

And anyone who looked closely at the picture in the throne room, could see two sets of mysterious footprints in the far corner of the painting where the mountains that stole your heart met the forests in a curtain of green, under clouds which sweetened the sky.

The End

Sometimes it is hard to accept sadness, whether it's your own or another's. Understanding the sadness of others is a kind of emotional skill.

Sadness meant that Notxa could not paint the works he was capable of, because grief weakens us, because dejection may deprive us of our better qualities. He had the luck to meet Miska, who understood him, gave him her support, and encouraged him.

Guilt

Guilt is being aware of having done something against ethical, legal, social, or religious principles. It is good to feel guilt for damage we have caused. When this happens, we must request forgiveness and repair the damage caused.

In every situation when we have done something wrong, we have to think: What could I have done to avoid it? But this must not lead us to feeling guilty all the time. There are people who feel guilty, but have done nothing bad. They have just made a mistake or something hasn't turned out as well as they wanted.

It is worth distinguishing between guilt and embarrassment. Embarrassment is the feeling we experience when something makes us look ridiculous to others.

The Stone Woman

A Legend from Vietnam

When the old fishermen of Lang Son tell this legend, they sometimes have been known to claim that it is a true story. It is such a fine story, however, that it may be better left as a legend. Imagine a family of country people, father, mother, son, and daughter.

The father and mother went to work in the fields while Van, the boy, and Thi, the girl, stayed at home.

"Behave yourselves," their parents said, kissing them on the cheek. "We will be back soon and we'll eat lunch together."

One morning, before leaving, the father told Van to finish peeling some sugar canes that stood behind the kitchen door. Sitting on a stool, the boy stripped off the leaves with a knife. Thi, the girl, was playing at her brother's feet when the knife slipped from Van's hands and fell on the girl's head. Van shuddered when he saw a trail of blood pouring under the black, curly hair of Thi, who fell on the floor in a faint.

Van was so frightened, he ran away because he was convinced he had hurt her badly.

"I must have killed her!" he thought, while he ran off not knowing where. He was trembling and crying; his heart was overflowing with sadness and fear.

That night he slept in the forest. At dawn he decided to walk to a nearby village. He reached a seaside town and, when he saw the port, he had an idea. "I know what I will do! I will stow away in the hold of the biggest ship I can find and travel far from home, to the other side of the sea."

The belly of the ship he found was dark. After a long while, when the ship had reached its destination, Van came out into the light. He was a very long way from his homeland (or at least he thought he was).

"Here they will not find me," he breathed out calmly.

Van signed on as a sailor and went from end to end of the Gulf of Tonkin and the South China Sea. But the sorrow at having killed his sister never left him; he felt guilty. How often nightmares took him back to that ill-fated morning and he awoke soaked in sweat! This memory always froze his smile. Could he ever be happy again?

The truth is that he had not hurt Thi as much as he thought. When their parents returned, they found her crying. They cleaned her wound, which was no more than a scratch on the skin. After a few days, the only sign of the wound was a scar that her hair

covered. But misfortunes never strike alone. One day while her parents were at work, some slave-trafficking pirates snatched her and took her to the north of the country, where they sold her to some rich landowners who made her their slave. They often sent her to the fish auction beside the harbor. One day a young, good-looking sailor kept staring at her.

"What a pretty girl! And what beautiful hair she has!"

He fell in love with her. They met each other for the week his ship was moored in the harbor. And later he always saw her when his ship anchored at that quay. Thi was also delighted by him. They spent long periods of time together. What a good time they had chatting and walking together! They began to draw up plans for their future.

"When your masters allow it, we will get married, we will look for a house near the beach, we will have children and we'll be happy all our lives," Van told her one spring day, when they were sitting by the river mouth.

Thi rested her head on his shoulder while he hugged her.

Van caressed her hair and…discovered a scar that made his heart turn over!

He got up, ran off, and took refuge in the most hidden corner of his ship.

The following morning, the ship went out to sea. Perhaps it went slower because of the overwhelming weight that Van carried in his chest: the young woman was his sister; he could not marry her.

Thi returned each day to the quay at sunset: she climbed up on the rocks and spent hours staring at the horizon. Each evening she stayed longer, until one day she did not return home. She had turned into a stone statue, the statue of a woman with her head raised, her look fixed on the distance, hoping for the return of her loved one.

The old fishermen of Lang Son will tell you that this is why they call that rocky crag *Hon vong phu*, which means "the woman who waits."

The End

We may feel guilty at times when we shouldn't, because we have not done anything as bad as we imagined, or we have done something without any bad intention. We have to overcome this feeling, because it doesn't do any good.

This is what happened in the story. Van felt excessively guilty for what he had done, since he had dropped the knife unintentionally, and he did not know that the girl he had fallen in love with was his sister.

Stamina and Recovery

The capacity for recovery after a difficult situation or any problem we face in life is called resilience. It is a word used in engineering and architecture to refer to construction materials that are both hard and flexible. For example, steel and concrete are resilient materials, whereas glass and lead are not.

Resilience applied to a person means the capacity to overcome very difficult situations, since he/she has the stamina to face up to unfavorable circumstances, but at the same time, is flexible enough to adapt. Faced with hostile situations, there are people who overcome them and others who do not. The former are resilient, they are able to recover from misfortunes and calamities, they can overcome them without giving in.

Aeneas and the Destruction of Troy

From Virgil's *Aeneid*
(Ancient Rome)

For ten years the city of Troy had been besieged by the Greek army that wanted to take it. After many attempts, the Greeks finally managed to enter the city. They built a huge wooden horse in which they hid many warriors and left it in front of the city walls.

The Trojans thought it was a present for their gods and took it inside the city, although some suspected it might be a trap. At night, all the Greek warriors inside came out, began to slaughter Trojans, and set the entire city on fire.

Aeneas, a Trojan general who lived in the city with all his family, took up his weapons, preparing to die at the enemy's hands. He brought together a group of young fighters and encouraged them by shouting, "Though it seems we are lost and everything is against us, follow me."

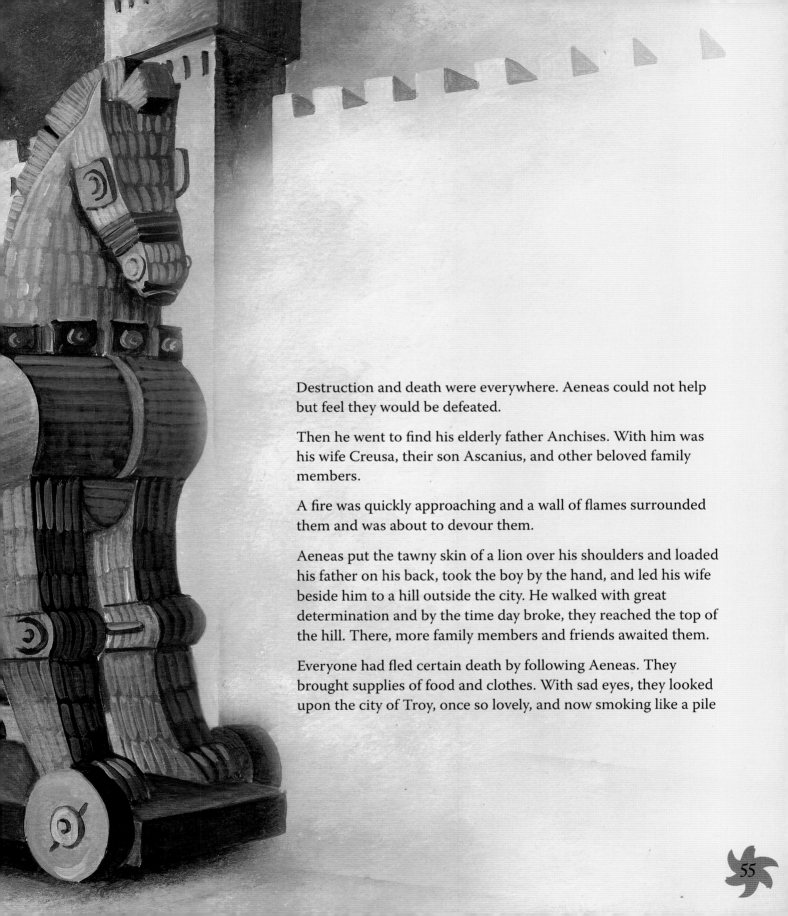

Destruction and death were everywhere. Aeneas could not help but feel they would be defeated.

Then he went to find his elderly father Anchises. With him was his wife Creusa, their son Ascanius, and other beloved family members.

A fire was quickly approaching and a wall of flames surrounded them and was about to devour them.

Aeneas put the tawny skin of a lion over his shoulders and loaded his father on his back, took the boy by the hand, and led his wife beside him to a hill outside the city. He walked with great determination and by the time day broke, they reached the top of the hill. There, more family members and friends awaited them.

Everyone had fled certain death by following Aeneas. They brought supplies of food and clothes. With sad eyes, they looked upon the city of Troy, once so lovely, and now smoking like a pile of ash, reduced to the remains of a bonfire. They were prepared to follow Aeneas wherever he wanted to go. They built boats and set out to sea on a very long journey that took them toward Italy, where, it is said, they founded Rome as a new Troy.

As you can see, resilience has a lot to do with the attitude we adopt toward life. There are people for whom everything seems bad or inadequate. There are others who try to see the positive side of life. This has to do with resilience—like metal that bends but can be straightened again.

Our Trojan hero, Aeneas, is an example, since through every adversity, he always pulled himself together and recovered his spirit.

Being Realistic

We all set goals for ourselves—you do too. If the goals are realistic, they are easier to achieve. Ones that are too easy do not motivate us and make personal growth harder; and ones that are too ambitious are usually not realistic. The balance between the two extremes must characterize the goals you set for yourself. You must "keep your feet on the ground."

At times, even though goals are realistic, they are not achieved. Then you feel frustrated. Frustration is the emotion we have when a barrier is placed between us and the goal we want to achieve.

You can experience frustration at disappointing situations: a soccer game in which you fail to score, an exam that you fail in spite of studying, an umbrella that won't open when it's raining cats and dogs, and an internet connection that goes down while you're on the computer.

The Three Fish

A Tale from the *Panchatantra* (India)

In a river of India, there were three fish that were close friends. One had silvery scales, another had red ones, and the third, yellow ones. If you want to imagine them, the first looked like bright silver, the second was reminiscent of a live flame of fire, and the third was pure gold. The brackish lagoon where they lived was very close to the ocean where the river spilled its waters: they could even taste the salt of the seawater when the tide came in.

One afternoon the silvery fish heard an old fisherman talking while he was mending his nets, "My fellow fishermen, the sea gives us good fish. We go out when the sun has just come up in the East and we return when it's at the highest point in the sky. Our boats come in loaded with fish. But I have seen that just before the river reaches the sea, the water there is full of freshwater fish, which are also tasty. Why don't we go up the river tomorrow and try to catch them?"

"Why not?" his friends replied. "We lose nothing by trying it."

As soon as the silvery fish heard this, he rushed to find the red and yellow ones. "Do you know what I heard the fishermen saying?" he asked his friends.

And then he told them every detail.

"What are these pack of rascals thinking?" the red fish replied, upset. "I'll teach those wretches a good lesson. My teeth are very sharp and I'll use them to gnaw through the net. And if they catch me…why, I'll bite their fingers! When they see how fearsome I am, they'll let me go and will be sorry for their boldness."

But the yellow fish was filled with dread. "It's useless!" he cried in resignation. "If this sad destiny is the one reserved for us, none of our efforts will work."

The silver fish didn't know how to respond, given the reactions of his two friends. He knew how different they were in their characters, but he hadn't expected them to react as they did, one so brave and one so cowardly.

"Please, let's think things through," the silver fish said. "The fishermen are much stronger than us. If we confront them, we'll end up losing. After the first fright we give them, they'll simply pull the nets up on deck and might even club us."

"That's why I said we should accept our lot patiently and not fight with them," the fish who looked like a thread of fine gold said.

"What you say doesn't seem sensible either, my friend," the fish that gleamed like silver said. "We have to do what we can. The immortal gods want us to stay calm and last

out the storm firmly. We have to find a solution. You know what we should do? Right now, let's swim up river as far from the sea as we can, swimming against the current. Then tomorrow at dawn they won't be able to catch us."

"Nothing too good can be written about a coward," the fish like fire reproached him. "And you're a coward from head to tail!"

"Let's not complicate the situation or it'll only be worse," the golden fish stated pessimistically.

Faced by the stubbornness of the red and yellow fish, the silvery fish, convinced that his decision was the most realistic one, said goodbye to his two friends with friendly taps of his tail.

The silvery fish had a premonition that he would not see them again. He began to swim upriver until there was not a speck of salt in the water and the riverbed was too shallow for the fishing boats to move easily.

The next morning the fishermen boarded their boats and went upriver to the place the old fisherman had spoken about. They cast their anchor and lowered their nets.

The red fish sunk its teeth into the ropes and gnawed at them with his teeth's steely tips. When they hoisted the fish on deck, he flung himself against the first fisherman who put out his hands to catch him. Very soon he felt a blow on the head that left him stunned.

The yellow fish lay still at the bottom of the net, as if he were dead.

"There's nothing to be done but give up!" he repeated in useless acquiescence.

Soon he lay beside the fish of fire.

The silvery fish continued swimming, submerged in the freshwater pools near the river's sources, where the boats would never come.

It is important to increase our frustration tolerance so that, though we experience disappointment, we are able to overcome it with no great problems. We must search for effective solutions.

The red fish responded with impossible goals; the yellow fish, with no goals at all; the silvery fish looked for a realistic, effective solution. You can see how it turned out for the three of them.

Making Responsible Decisions

It is true that we often think we make reasoned, logical decisions, but we almost always make decisions according to our emotional state or personal interests. Some of your decisions might be: what TV program will I watch today? What shall I do in my free time? Where will I spend my holidays? What will I be when I grow up? If you stop to think a little, you'll realize that in all these situations, emotions play a major role in our decisions.

When we realize how much our emotions can influence what we do, we can make better choices and be responsible for the decisions we make.

Without freedom there is no choice. But when I choose, I may make a mistake. I have to assume as well the responsibility for being wrong.

The Case of Señor Paso

A Tale by Esteve Pujol

Señor Paso was likeable, plump, and always good-humored. He had a very elegant black moustache and wavy gray hair. I knew him for many years and always believed him to be a decisive and strong-willed man.

One day I met him in the stands of a sports field, watching a junior athletics competition.

"How's it going, Señor Paso?" I greeted him.

"Wonderfully well, and recently still better," he replied with a broad smile.

"What do you mean 'recently still better'? Have you won the lottery, Señor Paso?"

"No," he said. "Something much better. I've given up smoking. It was a great decision. Congratulate me, young man!"

I shook his hand very warmly and added, "Congratulations. It is good news!"

Señor Paso, so friendly and plump, was a chain smoker. He lit one cigarette right after another; he was like a walking chimney. I don't know if the black of his moustache was natural or if it had darkened with cigarette smoke.

How could it be that someone who loved to smoke so much came to the conclusion that giving up smoking was a great decision?

"And how did you do it, Señor Paso? With a great deal of willpower, right?"

"You see, I'd made this resolution on several New Year's Eves. But in the end, it all boiled down to laughter."

"But what do you mean? By laughing you gave up smoking?"

"Look," he said. "I'll explain. I'd wanted to give up smoking for years. I'd tried everything: chewing gum, patches, sessions with psychiatrists….I can't even remember all the strategies I tried! I began to think that my willpower was so weak that I would never be able to do it. But I refused to accept this.

"I made a decision, a ridiculous one at that: whenever I lit a cigarette, I wouldn't finish it. Before I finished, I would put it out and throw it away. This way I'd smoke less and damage myself less. You see, it was quite a homemade system. Not even I was sure of its success. It was not exactly giving up, just smoking a bit less.

"But it worked. Each time I put out the cigarette a little bit earlier, until one day I found I was leaving half of it unsmoked. And so I kept on shortening the part that I smoked."

"I agree you can't call this giving up smoking, Señor Paso," I admitted.

"Wait, now comes the best part. A time arrived when I lit the cigarette and after a couple of puffs, I put it out and threw it away. It was ridiculous! When I saw myself lighting the cigarette and throwing it away immediately, I began to

laugh like an idiot. I said to myself, 'What a fool I am! Lighting cigarettes to put them out a second later!'

"I laughed and laughed. I laughed so hard that I never lit another one again. That's why I told you it was a 'question of laughter.' Sometimes big decisions happen like this—they don't always have to be made by promises, solemn oaths, or legally binding certificates."

And this, my friends, is the true story of Señor Paso.

The End

Like everyone, you have the intelligence to know what decisions have to be made, the willpower to make them, the memory to remember you have made them, and the friends to help you carry them out.

Señor Paso found it difficult to make an important decision, but he found a way of doing so. It is not always easy. All decisions, little or big, can affect our future. We can make decisions freely, but with responsibility.

Memories

Simple memories create emotions. You can have memories of successes and of failures. The former help you to move on ahead; the latter may paralyze you and prevent you from reacting.

With practice, you learn to do things well. If you remember what worked out well for you, it will always help you to reinforce the road you have taken, give you encouragement, and push you forward.

João's Leap

A Legend from the Amazon (Brazil)

Everyone knows the Amazon, South America's longest and widest river. There are a great many tributaries of all sizes that pour their waters into its basin. The legend of our hero takes place on one of them.

"João, you'll hurt yourself, you're too bold! Don't you see it's too wide?" his mother shouted to stop her ten-year-old son jumping across the stream in front of him. "Don't you see that you can't reach the other side by jumping and you'll fall in the water? You should cross it on the wooden plank further up; that's why it was put there."

"I can jump it, Mom, you'll see. I've done it before with room to spare," João replied.

He made a good running start and jumped it with a bit to spare. His face was full of satisfaction, which meant: "You see how far I can jump? I knew it!"

What long jumps he was capable of! Not even he suspected that one day he would become a hero precisely because of his jumping ability.

João was determined, as you've already seen, but from time to time, he had moments of doubt, like everyone of course. Sometimes he thought to himself, "I don't know if I can do it," as if fear had suddenly taken over his body. This happened once when his father, Inacio, told him to look after Fernando, his little brother, and take him to his Aunt Maria Luisa's house in the next village. But after he did, he realized there was nothing to be afraid of, so every time his father asked him to look after Fernando after that, he did it with ease.

João's village was small; everyone living there knew and helped each other. To keep the land fertile, the villagers set fire to the fields and buried the burnt stubble, which served as fertilizer for the next batch of crops. They did the same thing in some parts of the forest, in order to increase the amount of cultivated land they had. They knew how to control the fire so that it didn't spread further than they wanted it to.

João's family had a small plot where they grew vegetables, and another bigger one with bananas, rice, and cassava root. Their field ended on the bank of a stream that meandered this way and that, causing the water to dig a narrow, but deep, channel.

One summer day, Senhor Inacio decided to light a fire, as he often did. He started the task in the morning, with the help of his neighbors. Everything was going perfectly; they knew their work well. As the flames cleaned the field to prepare it for next year's harvest, they had no idea of the danger about to be unleashed upon them.

Suddenly the wind came up. It changed direction and the fire ran where it shouldn't. The field workers scrambled to correct the route of the flames. They did not realize that João and Fernando were playing on the other side of the stream, exactly the direction the hot flames of the fire were headed.

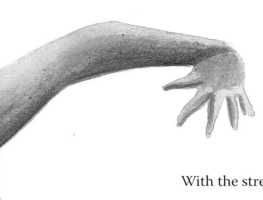

With the stream in front of them, João panicked.

"I won't be able to cross it. The ditch is too deep and, if I fall, I won't be able to climb out." But then he remembered and said to himself, "Yes, I can jump it, yes I can. I've done it on other occasions over even wider holes. If I've done it before, I'll do it now, too!"

João took some steps back, ran up, and leapt as far as he could…and still landed with a bit to spare! He hurried toward the adults, who were trying desperately to control the fire.

"Quickly! Fernando's waiting for me on the other side!"

They came at once. His little brother was weeping on the other bank because the flames were very close and he was afraid. The men feared that they wouldn't be able to reach him by jumping. They worried they wouldn't be able to do it.

"I'll jump and then you can throw me a rope," João shouted. "I've jumped it before and now I'll do it again."

Ignoring the warnings, he leapt again. The men threw him the rope, he caught it and he tied it to a tree trunk. Hanging onto the line and holding his brother, he crossed the flimsy but effective bridge to the other bank.

"Long live João, the brave boy!" they all shouted.

There is no need to describe how his parents kissed and hugged him. Senhor Inacio and Senhora Sonia were deeply moved, and so very proud of their brave son.

This is how the legend of "João's leap" started. They will still tell it to you, if you go to those parts.

Good memories are elements of life that give us energy:
"I was able to, I was happy, I did manage it….Now I can too."

João knew how to get the best out of good memories: his successes
helped him to achieve new ones. The legend does not focus on it,
but the country people too must have learned their lesson
from the uncontrolled fire.

Good memories are for returning to; bad ones, for learning and
not repeating them, so that they cause us as little harm as possible.

Empathy

Empathy is the capacity to put yourself in someone else's skin, to connect with the emotion the other person is feeling. If they tell you off, shout at you, or hit you, how do you feel? If you tell another person off, shout at, or hit him or her, how do you think he or she will feel?

Empathy requires emotional intelligence. It involves thinking about the whole situation: putting yourself in the other person's shoes, not only what he/she is thinking, but also what he/she is feeling.

Empathy is a factor in preventing conflicts and violence. At the same time, it assists happiness. It is an essential part of emotional intelligence. It is understanding the emotions and feelings of others.

75

The Bunch of Grapes

A Story by Leo Tolstoy (Russia)

In Russia there was a family of laborers who had a vine that gave them enough grapes to eat their fill and even make wine for their family and neighbors.

The father's name was Ivan Pavlovich. He had white hair and a white beard, and was usually calm. The mother's name was Lisabeta Prokofievna. She was diligent and serene, with rosy skin. Their five children sat round the table: Vladimir, age 20; Hippolyte, 18; Nastasia, the older of the girls, was 14; then came Aglaya, the most playful child, just 11; and the youngest of the family, Fyodor, was seven and a half.

One September day, the father went to the vine and saw a bunch of grapes that seemed to be saying, "Cut me." So he cut it.

When he had it between his fingers, he thought, "My good Lisabeta deserves this lovely bunch of grapes. I will give it to her." On getting home, he left the grapes on the table without saying anything.

Lisabeta knew that Ivan had left the grapes for her. When she was about to pluck the first grape, she thought, "Vladimir would very much like to eat this bunch when he comes back at midday. I'll leave them on his bed for him."

Vladimir smiled when he saw the grapes and, nearly at the point of eating them, thought better of it. "How good my mother is! I work a lot, but Hippolyte has to put up with the bad-tempered shopkeeper. I'll leave the bunch for him."

When Hippolyte saw the bunch, he knew at once it was a present from Vladimir. He would have swallowed them down in an instant, but he thought, "It infuriates me that Nastasia has such a bad time at the dressmaker's house. She'll like this bunch. I'll leave them for her in her room."

Nastasia jumped for joy and twirled round on her toes, she was so happy. "This is from Hippolyte," she thought. "My job is really not so bad. I have a good time with the customers. But Aglaya has to spend all day with a surly teacher. I will leave the grapes on her bedside table."

When Aglaya saw the grapes, she exclaimed, "Ay, Nastasia is so nice! But I'll give them to Fyodor, the baby of the house."

And Fyodor knew that it was Aglaya who had left them for him, but he said to himself, "My father spends all day working the land. He deserves these grapes."

When Ivan Pavlovich had that bunch in his hands again, he was moved. He lifted Fyodor up and kissed him.

Before supper, the father made a very short, but highly emotional speech, "Dear Lisabeta Prokofievna and children of my heart, how lucky we are! In thinking about others and in giving freely, we make them happy. And in doing this, we ourselves find happiness.

The End

People who have empathy do to others what they would like others to do to them. They know how others will feel, just as if they had experienced it. They do not treat people badly. They prefer others to feel good, because then they too will feel good.

The parents and children of the family in the story all wanted to eat the bunch of grapes, but they saw that, if they wanted to eat the fruit, then each of the others would like to, as well. And they acted responsibly.

Shyness

Shyness is a feeling that happens in certain situations. The person who experiences shyness behaves timidly and faintheartedly. Sometimes fear and anxiety accompany shyness. Everyone can experience it. Rather than talk of shy people, it is best to refer to situations that make someone shy. Anyone can feel this, for example, in social situations in which they feel awkward.

Some people are more prone to feeling shy; others have to be in a particular situation to experience it, for example, standing before an audience or appearing in any of the communications media.

People who are generally considered very intelligent, such as Jean-Jacques Rousseau, Napoleon, Agatha Christie, Alfred Hitchcock, Henry Miller, Orson Welles, or Jorge Luis Borges, were very shy but knew how to overcome it or live with it in an acceptable manner.

Cyrano de Bergerac

From the Play by Edmond Rostand (France)

In Saint-Béat, a town in France, situated on the bank of a curve in the Garonne River, the most noble houses rose above the whole town on Main Street. In one of these palaces lived a young woman named Roxanne. If you were to cross the hollow, you would easily reach the river. Here everything was dark and silent, no carts rattled along the cobbled streets. Here it was cold, and the damp of the Garonne penetrated your bones.

One evening Roxanne stepped onto her balcony to see Christian, a very handsome young man with whom she was in love. He was also in love with Roxanne and planned to tell her so tonight. He had to do it from the street without shouting too much, because her parents still did not let him enter the house.

To the right of the door, hidden behind a column and wrapped in a cape, was a gentleman with a sword. If you could see him, you would surely notice an enormous nose sticking out of a very ugly face. This soldier, Cyrano de Bergerac, was a poet who wrote love poems, and he too was secretly in love with Roxanne. What was he doing, hiding there? Well, his friend Christian had asked him to whisper pretty words that Christian planned to repeat aloud to Roxanne. Cyrano agreed to help Christian and to conceal his own love for Roxanne, because he thought that his very big nose would frighten her. Besides, Cyrano was timid, bashful, and incapable of declaring his love to so delicate and genteel a young lady.

In addition, Christian did not dare write to Roxanne, either, because he was not a good writer. He had Cyrano write the letters for him. You may have guessed by now that Cyrano agreed to write the letters because he himself was incapable of writing a single line to tell her that he loved her.

80

Several nights later, Christian once again came to Roxanne's balcony. Roxanne told him, "My love, in the beginning, I fell in love with you because I saw how good-looking you were. But then I heard you speak and read the letters you sent me, and now I have fallen in love with your soul. You have convinced me you are noble and a gentleman, and that you know how to express your feelings better than anyone. I love you, Christian."

Soon the two were married. The whole of Saint Béat dressed up for the festival, and the town erupted with joy during the days following the marriage, because the wedding parties of noble families lasted a week.

Poor Cyrano knew he had lost Roxanne forever.

But destiny decreed that the King of France should call Christian, who was a soldier, to war against a neighboring country. In the middle of the battle, an enemy bullet killed the handsome soldier.

When the news reached his wife Roxanne, she felt terrible grief. She could not believe that her beloved would not return from the war and she would never again have him beside her.

Desolate, she thought of seeking consolation with Christian's friend, our Cyrano with the long nose and homely looks. He would remind her of the excellent qualities of his friend, the values that adorned him, his talent as a poet.

Cyrano could not refuse. Confused and embarrassed, he set off for Roxanne's house. On the way, some bandits attacked him to steal his money. A good swordsman, Cyrano defended himself and put the ruffians to flight, but he was very badly wounded.

Determined to reach Roxanne despite his injuries, he reached the house where Roxanne awaited him. She begged him with tears in her eyes to read the last love letter that Christian had written her. Cyrano started to read it with all the tender and affectionate feeling that those lines could express. But without

realizing, he raised his eyes from the paper and recited from memory, word for word, everything that the text said. Do you think he would forget what he himself had written? The words sprung from his heart, even though he could never say them aloud.

Roxanne, realizing what this meant, ran to embrace Cyrano. But she reached him too late. The long-nosed gentleman had died from the mortal wounds inflicted by the bandits. Too late for Roxanne and too late for Cyrano de Bergerac.

So when you go to Saint Béat, where the Garonne enters France, ask for the house of Roxanne and they will show you where it is. You may see, behind the column, the shadow of a man with a long nose.

The End

Shyness can cause us serious difficulties in relating to others.

It really caused our Cyrano enormous hardship.

One must overcome shyness with willpower and decisiveness.
Personal effort will always help you greatly.

Vengeance

Vengeance means causing harm to someone in response to an offense committed by that person.

When you feel offended or hurt by someone or something, you want to avenge yourself, as everyone does. But vengeance is negative and dangerous. If we govern ourselves by the rule "An eye for an eye, a tooth for a tooth," we would all be blind and toothless. Taking vengeance on someone is causing him/her damage as a response to the damage we have received.

Never confuse vengeance with justice. Justice is a virtue; vengeance is a defect.

For there to be justice, we cannot be at the same time judge and prosecutor. A judge must be impartial. In vengeance, there is no justice, but uncontrolled violence.

The Vengeance of Achilles

From Homer's *Iliad* (Ancient Greece)

The *Iliad*, a book written very long ago, narrates adventures of every kind. Here is one of the more beautiful ones.

There was a very brave and powerful warrior, very fast and invincible, whose name was Achilles. He was a general of the Greek armies who wanted to conquer the great city of Troy.

The King of Troy was called Priam. He was a very wise old man, greatly loved by the Trojans. Of all his children, there was one, Hector, who was like the king himself had been when he was young. Hector's father placed all his hopes in his son. Hector was his favorite.

Hector and Achilles hated each other profoundly. In the hearts of the two generals, the desire for vengeance grew. Achilles' hatred surpassed all bounds when Hector killed his best friend, Patroclus, whom Achilles loved more than if he were his own brother.

One day what never should have happened did happen. The great Achilles and Hector confronted each other. When the two were exhausted, Achilles won: Hector lost his life.

As was the custom, Achilles carried Hector's body to his tent near the beach, where the Greeks' fleet was moored.

Poor Priam was told that his beloved son Hector had died and that Achilles had carried him off as if he were a trophy! Added to this loss was yet another pain: he would not be able to bury him with all the honors that so brave a general deserved.

What was Priam to do? He had an idea. With all a father's love, he would go to see Achilles in his tent and ask him to return Hector's body. When Priam found himself before his enemy, he knelt at Achilles' feet, embraced the warrior's knees with tears in his eyes and said, "Achilles, I recognize all the damage and suffering we Trojans have caused you. A short time ago, Hector killed Patroclus, your best friend. If you wanted, you could kill me right now. I ask you to grant me the greatest of favors: return the body of my son to me."

Achilles was moved to see how much Priam loved Hector. And he replied:

"King Priam," he said, "eat with me now and spend the night here. At dawn I will order that Hector's body be wrapped in silks and you can take the body of the son you loved so much to Troy."

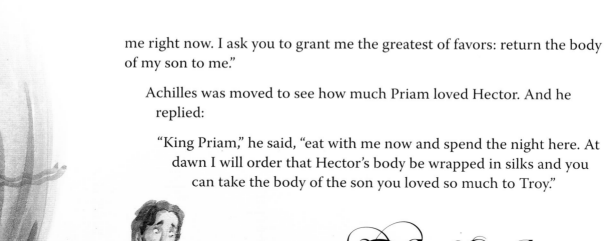

The End

Vengeance is paying back in the same coin, entering you into a spiral of never-ending violence. This cycle of growing cruelty has to be broken. The feeling of vengeance must not spill into violence, but into the search for justice. This is why we need responses other than vengeance. The story of Achilles and Priam gives us a hint.

Assertiveness

Assertiveness may be a new word for some of you. It refers to the ability to express your opinions and rights directly, without denying or questioning the opinions or rights of others.

You can distinguish between aggressive, passive, and assertive behavior. An example of aggressive behavior is someone thinking: "I'm right and you're wrong; so shut up and listen to me; you'll get it if you don't do what I say…" You can imagine that this behavior does not help you build relationships with other people.

At the other extreme is passive behavior, for example, someone thinking: "My opinion doesn't matter and interests no one. Maybe what I say or do, especially if I protest, won't please the other person, and then I'll have to suffer the consequences. So it's better that I shut up and suffer in silence."

The two kinds of behaviors are inappropriate extremes in interpersonal and social relationships. You have to find a balance between the two. Assertive behavior is what is appropriate.

Aggressive and passive behaviors are impulsive and spontaneous, whereas assertive behavior has to be learnt.

Some Do It Like This and Others, Like That

A Tale by Esteve Pujol

Allow me to introduce you to Elena. She was a brave and decisive woman, and even a bit quarrelsome. One Monday, as she was so very fond of doing every Monday, Elena sat at a restaurant table and asked the waiter for a rare steak, one that was a little raw. She liked them like that: everything, after all, is a question of taste.

When the waiter brought out her meal, it turned out that the steak was not at all rare; rather, it looked like a big piece of burnt charcoal!

"Excuse me, young man," Elena said in a most haughty tone of voice. "Do you see what you've brought me? Do you treat all the restaurant's customers like this? It's not surprising there are so few people in this restaurant! You should be ashamed! I've never seen such a sight! You call this a rare steak? Call the chef at once because I want to speak with him. Or is there no one in charge? They call any old place a restaurant nowadays! Take this away and return it to the kitchen! And bring me what I asked for!"

Now I introduce you to Clara. She, on the other hand, was quite timid, very conscious of herself, insecure, fearful, a little weak, and all in all, rather shy.

90

On this same Monday, Clara sat at a restaurant table—not at the same place as Elena, but another one! Strangely enough, she too asked for a rare steak, just like the previous Elena.

When the waiter brought it, the steak was not at all rare; rather it looked like a big piece of burnt charcoal!

Clara looked at the steak. She did not look at the waiter, she did not raise her eyes from her plate. Instead, she began to eat the steak, and while she ate it, she thought to herself, "Don't cause any problems, don't cause any problems! Don't say anything, because this good man (one has to recognize that the waiter has the face of a good man) might get angry and, in the end, I'll be the one who loses. After all, what does it matter whether the steak is rare or well done? I'll eat it and that's that."

And she ate it, not all at once, although she did grumble a bit, but only under her breath.

Now I introduce you to Mar. One might classify her as a normal, balanced person, neither aggressive nor excessively shy, but just right, like a meal with just the right amount of seasoning. She knew what she was worth, which was a lot, and controlled herself as necessary, which was enough.

And on the same Monday, the very same Monday, Mar was also sitting at a table in a restaurant; another restaurant, different from Elena's or Clara's. And imagine that, she also ordered a rare steak and you already know what happened. The waiter brought it to her, and it turned out that the steak was not at all rare; rather it looked like a big piece of burnt charcoal!

Well, Mar looked at the waiter, smiled at him, and said in a gentle voice—remember Mar was in a restaurant and in restaurants it is not polite to shout—"Please, I think this is not quite how I ordered the steak. If you consult your notebook, you will see that I asked for it rare. I understand that, with so many orders at lunchtime, perhaps it's been confused with another table's steak. It can happen to all of us on occasion. I ask you to bring me the steak as I ordered it. Thank you."

Elena, the one who had screamed and shouted, was quite right not to return to that restaurant: the waiter had an excellent memory for faces.

Clara, the too-shy one, didn't go back, either. She looked for another restaurant, and perhaps she's still looking.

Mar did go back. Why not? Plus, it was close to her job. The waiter always greeted her with a very welcoming smile…because he too had a good memory for faces.

The End

Elena was aggressive, quarrelsome, and verbally violent. When things didn't turn out as she wanted, she attacked like a wounded animal. Clara gave up too easily. She let herself be walked on, and when things didn't go as she wanted, she hid in her shell. However, Mar defended her rights calmly. When things were not as she thought they should be, she spoke up politely. You see the results.

We have to be assertive, but avoid counter-productive aggression and useless passivity.

Gratitude

Gratitude is an emotion "in danger of extinction." Gratitude is to show recognition to someone who has done something positive for you, without expecting anything in return. It implies awareness of what others do for you. It also requires empathy in order to understand how this person will feel when you show your gratitude.

Expressing gratitude effectively requires preparation. You have to be conscious of its importance and appropriateness, look for the right place and time, and create the right environment, which sometimes will be in private and other times in public.

Often, expressing gratitude means overcoming certain emotional barriers related to embarrassment and shyness.

Haarlem, Grateful City

A Legend from the Low Countries

The Low Countries, in the North of Europe, are called this because much of their land is below sea level. Little by little, they have won land from the sea. The people there have raised some formidable walls, the dykes, so that the ocean does not run inland. In making the sea take a step back, now they have more room for their cities and tulip fields.

Can you imagine what would happen if a dyke broke? Undoubtedly, seawater would flood towns, cities, and crops, and many of their inhabitants would be drowned.

One autumn evening, in the city of Haarlem, Han Brinker, a blonde, alert eight-year-old, asked his parents, Raff and Brigitte, to let him take some cakes to Vincent, a blind man who lived half an hour away on foot. The parents agreed and Han, happy as a boy could be, walked along the street with the basket of cakes and a song on his lips.

Raff, Hans's father, was in charge of opening and closing the gates that regulated the water entering the canals that served as communication routes inside the city. Canals often served as the streets and avenues of many Dutch cities. Frequently, Hans had heard him say, "God protect us from any leak in a dyke! The strength of the sea would soon blow out the hole, however small it was, and it would become a breach. Soon the whole dyke would collapse and Haarlem would be submerged under the waters."

After spending quite a time keeping Vincent, the blind man, company, Hans returned home. He decided to take the long way around along a path beside the dyke. The sky had darkened and a fine rain began to fall. Over the sea, lightning bolts crackled out of the thick, black clouds.

Suddenly Hans heard a persistent whistling that seemed to come from the center of the dyke. He looked for the source of the noise and saw with horror a gush of

water coming through the wall.
The words of his father came to mind,
"God protect us from any leak in a
dyke!…Haarlem would be submerged under
the waters."

Hans left the empty basket on the ground and
climbed up the dyke's stones until he reached the hole
that the water was flowing through. What could he cover it
with? He could only think of using his finger—for the crack was
very tiny!—and so this is what he did. The flow of water stopped,
but he could not take his finger out or go for help, because otherwise
the water would flow in again.

"Raff, why hasn't Hans come back?" Brigitte asked her husband.

"It's raining hard, so he must have stayed to sleep at Vincent's house. He's done so before. Tomorrow morning he'll be here for breakfast," her husband replied.

The cold and damp were slowly starting to put Hans's body to sleep. He could hardly feel his fingers anymore and could not move his arms or legs.

"I mustn't take my finger out! The whole of Haarlem would be drowned by the seawater!" he repeated to himself in a whisper. "I mustn't take my finger out!"

Early in the morning, a priest on his way to St. Bavo's church saw Hans half asleep, but still covering the hole in the dyke.

"Hans, what are you doing up there? Come down at once!"

"I can't, sir. If I take my finger out, Haarlem will disappear beneath the waters," he said in a thin voice.

The priest ran off to tell Hans's parents and seek help. Raff and Brigitte arrived first. They and some bricklayers on their way to work helped Hans come down off the dyke and covered the hole. Some dry clothes, the heat of the hearth, and a cup of hot soup, returned the pinkness to his cheeks and movement to his sore limbs.

Imagine the party that Haarlem's inhabitants organized for Hans when they learned of his heroic deed. Everyone thanked him again and again for what he had done. If you go to Haarlem or other nearby towns, you'll find monuments dedicated to our hero. You will see him up on the dyke, covering the hole with a finger where the water was coming through.

The End

How easy it is to be grateful! How fantastic it is to be grateful! The city of Haarlem and its neighboring towns showed, and still show, their gratitude to Hans Brinker, a blonde, eight-year-old boy, whose alertness saved them from a terrible disaster.

Every monument they have raised to him and every time they tell this story, it is as if they were saying, "Thank you, Hans!"

Being grateful is a duty.

Forgiveness

Forgiveness is a highly complex and difficult emotion, thought, and behavior, especially when great damage has been caused. It is nothing like bumping into someone and saying "Oh sorry, I didn't see you."

To forgive (*for-give*) means to give something completely and entirely. It means you have put behind you completely an offense, a demand, a punishment…or the indignation or anger that certain situations or attitudes caused you, and it means "freeing" the guilty party from his/her obligation or mistake.

Forgiving is the complete opposite of vengeance; and forgiving does not mean renouncing justice.

Forgiveness rises from a very profound internal emotion, by which we eventually think: "although I feel deeply hurt, I am prepared to make you a gift."

Hatred and Forgiveness

From Romeo and Juliet by William Shakespeare (England)

In the city of Verona, in northern Italy, two rival families lived, the Montagues and the Capulets, who had hated each other profoundly for generations. Romeo, the oldest Montague son, snuck into a masked ball in the Capulet palace and fell in love with Juliet, the daughter of the house. An impossible love, as you'll see.

Romeo and Juliet married in secret; only Friar Lawrence, who married them, knew about it.

The undying hatred between the families was the cause of endless fights and challenges. In one of these street brawls, Juliet's cousin Tybalt and Romeo insulted and fought with each other: Tybalt was killed by Romeo.

When the Prince of Verona, who wanted peace for his city, found out, he condemned Romeo to exile forever. Romeo went to Mantua, some distance from Verona.

Count Paris, a relation of the Prince, wanted to marry Juliet. Remember that no one knew she was already married to Romeo. The young woman went to the Franciscan monastery to ask Friar Lawrence for advice. The good friar thought up a risky solution, "Juliet, as I am very skilled in herbal medicines and know all their virtues, I'll prepare a potion for you, so that you'll sleep for forty-two hours after you drink it and it will look as if you were dead. We will make all Verona think you really have died. Then I will send a message to Romeo, so that he knows you are alive, and he will come to fetch you from the mausoleum where you will be resting and both of you can slip away to Mantua."

Juliet accepted the proposal despite the fear it inspired in her.

You can imagine how sad the Capulets felt to hear that Juliet had died! They carried her to the family's mausoleum, to await burial a few days later, as was customary.

However, things become complicated! When Friar Lawrence's messenger approached Mantua, the city's sentries refused to let him in. But the news of Juliet's death did reach Romeo, who wanted to go and see her one last time and then die beside her. He left Mantua, arrived at Verona, and entered the mausoleum. There he found Count Paris weeping for Juliet. They both pulled their swords from their scabbards and Paris was killed. Romeo then took the fast-acting poison that he had brought in a flask and died embracing his beloved.

Meanwhile, the potion that made Juliet appear dead wore off, just as Friar Lawrence had planned. When she awoke, imagine her despair on seeing the corpse of her husband. Mad with grief, she seized the dagger from Romeo's belt and plunged it into her heart.

The Prince entered the mausoleum, accompanied by the Capulets and Montagues, and there they found the three bodies, of Romeo, Juliet, and Paris.

Friar Lawrence explained the whole story, as only he knew all the parts.

Then their eyes and hearts were opened.

"Capulet, Montague the Prince cried. "See what a scourge is laid upon your hate, that heaven finds means to kill your joys with love!"

"O brother Montague," Capulet said. "Give me your hand...for no more can I demand."

"But I can give you more. In Verona, I will raise a statue made of pure gold in memory of Juliet, your daughter. No monument will ever equal it," Montague replied.

"And I'll raise another one just as rich in memory of Romeo," Capulet added.

Finally, the Prince concluded, taking both of them by the hand,

A glooming peace this morning with it brings.
The sun for sorrow will not show his head,
Go hence, to have more talk of these sad things;
Some shall be pardon'd, and some punished;
For never was a story of more woe
Than this of Juliet and her Romeo.

The End

*It is important to learn to forgive. It makes you feel good,
much better than vengeance, rage, or hatred.*

*It was very hard for the Montagues and Capulets to find reconciliation.
They paid very dearly for their hatred, but forgiveness was the only way of continuing
to live in the same city, of remaking their families, of achieving peace. Only forgiveness
could insure that so sad a love story never be repeated. To forgive is to begin again.*

Sharing Emotions

Sharing emotions with others is a source of happiness for us and for them. It is possibly the highest and most pleasing part of humans living alongside each other.

Making others take part in our feelings effectively involves emotional awareness, an ability to name emotions, emotional control, empathy, assertiveness, and overcoming shyness.

We cannot share our emotions with everyone. We must learn to choose the right people to share them with and the right time to share them.

The Window

Anonymous

Rosa and Isabel shared a room in Torres del Río Hospital. They were both ill and had to spend a long time in the hospital. Luckily for Rosa, the doctors let her sit for a couple of hours each afternoon in the armchair beside her bed, near the window. Isabel was not so fortunate. She had to stay in bed on her back all the time, as her illness did not allow her to move. She could only stare at the ceiling of her room.

However, no one could stop them talking and talking about their families, their children, grandchildren, of the jobs they once had, of what they still dreamed of doing in life…the joys and suffering they had lived through, the hopes in their hearts….

"Isabel, do you want me to tell you what's happening in the street?" Rosa asked.

"Of course I do. What can you see through the window?"

"Well, now there's a couple with a curly-haired boy in a stroller; and over there, two lads talking and gesturing excitedly; and, near them, a very elegant young man is walking by."

"My boy Ginés," Isabel said, "had curly hair when he was little. And my husband also gestured a lot when he talked, and…elegant, well he was elegant."

"Now a lot of people are coming out of the subway station, and a lady with a bunch of flowers is passing, and a group of boys are running, and two policemen are riding on a motorcycle. Two elderly people are walking arm in arm…."

In this way, Rosa described everything going on in the street. Isabel was very pleased and her comments made Rosa happy.

Day after day, even though she couldn't see anything, Isabel enjoyed the scenes that Rosa communicated in vivid detail. It was as if Isabel was watching a film projected onto the ceiling that Rosa narrated with enthusiasm and care.

"Look, Isabel, today there is a big festival. Soon the procession will be here. Yes, now it's coming in from the other side of the square. Can you hear the music, Isabel? It's like a waltz. There are people dressed up like giants with big heads, dancing and jumping and teasing people. The municipal band is wearing its dress uniform. It's such a happy day!"

"At festivals," Isabel added, "Juan and I danced. He was a great dancer and I wasn't too bad myself. We loved to go with our boy and girl through the decorated streets. What else can you see, Rosa?"

"Now there are three fire engines with people tossing candy for the kids. Boys and girls dressed in traditional clothes are with them. I bet they're going to the town hall, where the mayor will receive them."

One morning toward the end of autumn, the nurses came in with breakfast for the two patients and to change their sheets. They discovered that Rosa, who was beside the window, had died peacefully during the night.

That afternoon, Isabel asked the nurse, "I'd like to ask a favor, Miss. Could you move me to the bed where Rosa was? There I'll be by the window and now that I'm able to sit up, I'd like to look out."

The ward nurse agreed readily. When she left the room, Isabel managed to prop herself up and look through the window. What she saw amazed her: the window faced a narrow patio and only looked out onto a gray wall!

"Miss," Isabel asked the nurse at suppertime, "why was Rosa telling me everything that was going on in the street and the square? She could only see a gray wall through the window!"

"Well, I don't know, Miss Isabel. She couldn't have seen anything but this wall."

The End

Rosa and Isabel, the characters in the story, shared emotions and memories, beauty and goodness. They made each other happy with a generous sprinkling of feelings. It was a marvelous story shared by the two of them. They lived together in joy.

Sayings and Quotations

Know thyself.
Proverb inscribed on the temple of the Oracle of Delphi

Only in searching for words, do we find thoughts.
Joseph Joubert, French philosopher

Self-control is the highest form of control.
Seneca, Roman philosopher

Beauty is nothing more than the promise of happiness.
Stendhal, French writer

Time cools, time clarifies; no mood can be maintained quite unaltered through the course of hours.
Mark Twain, writer from the United States

Anger is the start of madness.
Cicero, Roman orator and philosopher

Who trembles before any bush will not enter the forest.
Medieval proverb

With happiness, we are all more handsome.
Medieval proverb

I forgive myself.
Horace, Roman poet

The tongue resists because it is soft; teeth break because they are hard.
Chinese proverb

Things and people are not what we want them to be or what they appear to be. They are what they are.

Epictetus, Greek philosopher

Resolve and thou art free.

Henry Longfellow, poet from the United States

God gave us memories that we might have roses in December.

J. M. Barrie, British author

May I do to others as I would that they should do unto me.

Plato, Greek philosopher

In order for one to learn the important lessons of life, one must first overcome a fear each day.

Ralph Emerson, American writer

The best revenge is to be unlike him who performed the injury.

Marcus Aurelius, Roman emperor and philosopher

Let your "Yes" mean "Yes," and your "No" mean "No."

Matthew 5:37

Gratitude is the most exquisite form of courtesy.

Jacques Maritain, French philosopher

And if I were thy nurse, thy tongue to teach, "Pardon" should be the first word of thy speech.

William Shakespeare, English writer

Trouble shared is trouble halved. Joy shared is joy doubled.

Popular saying

A Child's Book of
Emotions

...contains twenty tales relating to each of these
twenty indispensable emotions:
I know myself, Naming emotions, Self-control, Enjoying beauty,
Being impulsive, Anger, Fear, Sadness, Guilt, Stamina and recovery,
Being realistic, Making responsible decisions, Memories,
Empathy, Shyness, Vengeance, Assertiveness, Gratitude,
Forgiveness, and Sharing emotions.